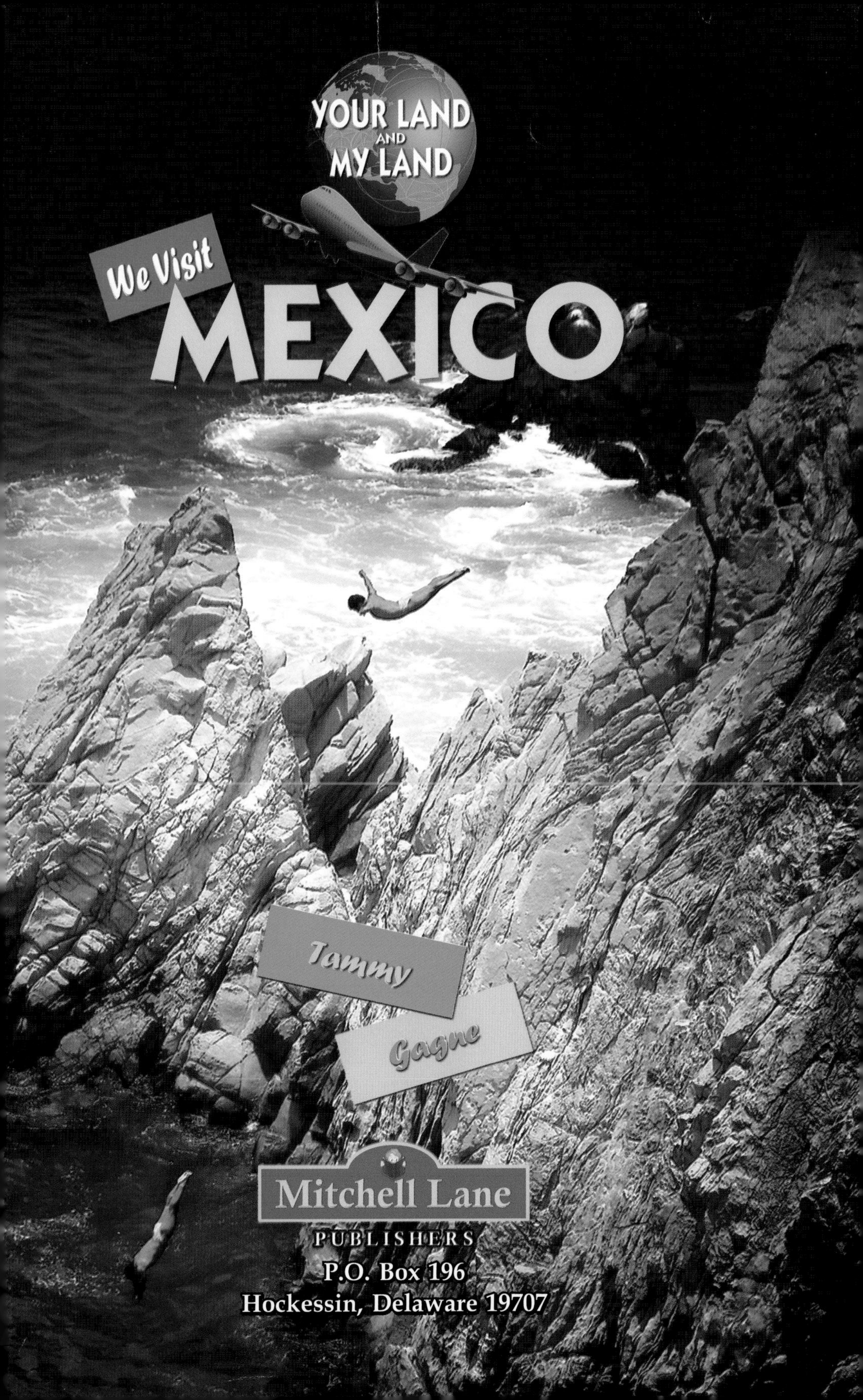

YOUR LAND
AND
MY LAND

We Visit

MEXICO

Tammy

Gagne

Mitchell Lane
PUBLISHERS
P.O. Box 196
Hockessin, Delaware 19707

YOUR LAND
AND
MY LAND

Brazil
Chile
Colombia
Cuba
Dominican Republic
Mexico
Panama
Puerto Rico
Peru
Venezuela

YOUR LAND
AND
MY LAND

We Visit
MEXICO

Mitchell Lane
PUBLISHERS

Printing   1   2   3   4   5   6   7   8   9

Library of Congress Cataloging-in-Publication Data
Gagne, Tammy.
  We visit Mexico/by Tammy Gagne.
      p. cm. — (Your land and my land)
  Includes bibliographical references and index.
  ISBN 978-1-58415-889-9 (library bound)
  1. Mexico—Juvenile literature. I. Title.
  F1208.5.G326 2010
  972—dc22
                                                          2010019386

PUBLISHER'S NOTE: This story is based on the author's extensive research, which she believes to be accurate. Documentation of this research is on page 61.

    The Internet sites referenced herein were active as of the publication date. Due to the fleeting nature of some web sites, we cannot guarantee they will all

Contents

Introduction

The area called Latin America consists of the North, Central, and South American countries that lie to the south of the United States—places such as Brazil, Cuba, Panama, and Venezuela. When most people think of these countries, they think of scorching hot weather, spicy foods, and Spanish-speaking people. If you visit these countries, you will indeed encounter most of these things, but you may also find areas with milder temperatures, eat delectable sweets, and hear numerous romance languages spoken. It all depends on exactly where you go.

In addition to providing the rest of the world with a number of exciting vacation spots, Latin America is home to more than 500 million people. Each nation has its own unique culture, economy, geography, and government. Latin America is also filled with ancient ruins, breathtaking landscapes, and exotic wildlife. This book is an introduction to Mexico, a beautiful country with a fascinating past and a challenging future.

Plaza de Armas,
Durango

The Regions and Countries of Latin America

Caribbean: Cuba, the Dominican Republic, and
   Puerto Rico
North America: Mexico
Central America: Belize, Costa Rica, El Salvador,
   Guatemala, Honduras, Nicaragua, Panama
South America: Argentina, Bolivia, Brazil, Chile,
   Colombia, Ecuador, Guyana, Paraguay, Peru,
   Suriname, Uruguay, Venezuela

LATIN
AMERICA

Guanajuato is perched in the central highlands of Mexico. Portions of the film *Once Upon a Time in Mexico*, starring Antonio Banderas and Selma Hayek, were filmed in Guanajuato.

Just South of the Border

Welcome to Mexico! Located just across the southern border of the United States, Mexico is a land rich in history, culture, and strife. Poverty and crime run rampant in some parts of Mexico. Mexico City, the capital, has one of the highest crime rates in the world. Still, the natural beauty of this country cannot be eclipsed by its struggles. From the magnificent mountain ranges to the turquoise waters of its tourist-filled beaches, Mexico is one of the most intriguing places on earth.

Many fascinating people have hailed from Mexico. Some names are instantly recognizable. Frida Kahlo, for example, was one of the greatest artists of the twentieth century. Salma Hayek, the Mexican-born actress who played Frida in the movie of the same name about the painter, is a star in her own right. You may have seen Hayek on the popular television series *Ugly Betty,* a show that she also produced. Other popular actors of Mexican descent include Jessica Alba, George Lopez, and Disney Channel's Selena Gomez and Demi Lovato.

The list of famous Mexican-Americans hardly ends there, though. It also includes Anthony Quinn, who was the first Mexican-born actor to win an Academy Award. Well-known sports heroes of Mexican heritage include football quarterback Tony Romo and boxer Oscar De La Hoya. Musician Carlos Santana was born in Mexico in 1947. The son of a mariachi violinist, Santana began his musical career playing the violin with his father's band on the streets of Tijuana. He began playing the guitar around the time his family moved to San Francisco, California, in the 1960s.

Rodolfo Neri Vela

Of course not all Mexicans who have done great things have become household names. You may not be familiar with Rodolfo Neri Vela or Ellen Ochoa, for instance. In 1985 Vela became the first Mexican-born astronaut. Ochoa became the first Hispanic woman in space just six years later. Other milestones made by brave Mexicans have less happy endings but an equally significant impact on history. Lori Ann Piestewa, a soldier whose mother was Mexican, served in the U.S. military. She was the first U.S. woman killed in the Iraq War.

Mexico and the United States haven't always gotten along smoothly. Despite working very hard, Mexican people face a constant struggle to earn enough money to care for their families. The United States, on the other hand, is one of the wealthiest nations in the world. Many Mexicans feel compelled to cross the border to the United States in hopes of making their lives better. Unfortunately, many do so illegally, even selling drugs as a way of supporting themselves. At times, problems like drug trafficking and illegal immigration have made relations between these neighboring countries difficult.

Ellen Ochoa

USA Mexico
Border at San Diego-Tijuana

Located in Chihuahua, the Naica Mine contains lead, silver, and zinc. In addition to these conventional metals, the Naica miners have found some of the largest selenite crystals ever discovered. Some sections have measured approximately 4 feet (1.2 meters) in diameter and 50 feet (15.2 meters) in length.

One thing that does seem to work well between Mexico and the United States is trade. There's a good chance that you use products made in Mexico every day. Tin, sugar, and natural gas are among Mexico's most commonly exported items to the United States. With its abundant mines, Mexico is also a large producer of the world's copper, gold, lead, salt, silver, and zinc. About one-sixth of the world's silver comes from Mexico. Even higher on the list of Mexico's top exports to the United

FYI FACT:

The North American Free Trade Agreement, known more commonly as NAFTA, went into effect January 1, 1994. This partnership between the U.S., Canada, and Mexico removed taxes on exports among the three countries. As a result of NAFTA, Mexico's trade with the U.S. and Canada has nearly tripled.

WHERE IN THE WORLD IS MEXICO?

N Mexico

Tijuana
Mexicali
Ciudad Juárez
Hermosillo
Chihuahua
Baja California
UNITED STATES
Pacific
Torreón
Monterrey
Matamoros
Gulf of Mexico
Culiacán
La Paz
Durango M E X I C O
Ocean
Mazatlán
Ciudad Victoria
Aguascalientes Guanajuato Tampico
Tabasco
Tula
Isla Mujer
Mérida Canc
Puerto Guadalajara
Cozum
Vallarta
Morelia
Mexico
Yucatán
Netzahualcóyotl Puebla
Veracruz
Villahermosa GUAT. BE
Acapulco Oaxaca
Chiapas
H

Where in the World

Mexico lies just south of the United States and extends to the northern border of Central America. The river that forms the border between Mexico and the United States has two names. In Mexico it is called the Río Bravo, but in the United States it is called the Rio Grande.

States, though, are oil and passenger cars. Oil is a billion-dollar industry in Mexico. You may not know of any Mexican car brands, but companies such as Ford and Volkswagen have factories in Mexico that produce vehicles, car parts, and accessories.

MEXICO FACTS AT A GLANCE

Crested caracara

Full Official name: United Mexican States (Mexico)

Size: 758,446 square miles (1,964,375 square kilometers)

Population: 111,211,789 (July 2009 est.)

Capital: Mexico City (population: over 20 million)

Highest point: Volcan Pico de Orizaba 18,700 feet (5,700 meters)

Lowest point: Laguna Salada, 32 feet below sea level (–10 meters)

Ethnic groups: Mestizo (Amerindian-Spanish) 60%, Amerindian 30%, white 9%, other 1%

Religious groups: Roman Catholic 77%, Protestant 6%, other 17%

Languages: Spanish, English, indigenous languages

Climate: Hottest month—July   Coolest Month—February

Agricultural products: corn, wheat, soybeans, rice, beans, cotton, coffee, fruit, tomatoes; beef, poultry, dairy products; wood products

Exports: manufactured goods, oil and oil products, silver, fruits, vegetables, coffee, cotton

Imports: metalworking machines, steel mill products, agricultural machinery, electrical equipment, car parts for assembly, repair parts for motor vehicles, aircraft, and aircraft parts

Flag: The modern Mexican flag was adopted in 1968. The government does not dictate what the colors stand for, but most people interpret the colors as follows: The green stripe signifies hope (or the independence movement). The white stripe stands for purity. The red stripe represents either religion or the blood the Mexican people have shed fighting for their freedom. The coat of arms represents the Aztec heritage and the legend of the founding of Mexico City.

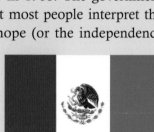

National flower: Dahlia pinnata

National bird: Crested caracara

Source: *CIA World Factbook,* Mexico

The National Museum of Anthropology features some striking sculptures. The jaguar played a large role in the culture and religion of the Olmec civilization. The animal was a mythological symbol of authority and proficiency in both hunting and battle.

A Colorful History

People have lived in the area we now call Mexico for as many as 20,000 years. The earliest of these inhabitants were hunters. Around 7000 BCE, the people of Mexico learned how to grow corn, and agriculture became the most common way of life. Farming provided the people with a more predictable source of food. Because they didn't have to spend so much time hunting, they had time to improve their lives in other ways. They developed societies with industry, government, and religion—all the important parts of a civilization.

Several civilizations have risen and fallen in the land of Mexico over the last 9,000 years. These include the Olmec, the Teotihuacán, the Toltec, the Maya, and the Aztec civilizations. Ruins from all of these historic time periods still stand in many areas of the country.

The Olmecs

The Olmecs inhabited Mexico as early as 1200 BCE. These people farmed the land that is now Veracruz and Tabasco, near the Gulf of Mexico. Very little is known about the Olmecs, but huge stone figures of human heads believed to have been built by them can still be found in this area. Most historians think that the Olmecs were indigenous to Mexico, but some believe they may have come from Africa instead. They think the giant statues look more like Africans than Mexicans.

Temple steps and pyramids at Teotihuacán. In the distance sits the Pyramid of the Sun, the world's third largest pyramid. When they were built more than 2,000 years ago, Mexican pyramids were plastered and painted red. None of the red coloring remains.

The Teotihuacáns

The Teotihuacán civilization began around 200 BCE. These people occupied the area near what is now Mexico City. At its peak, the Teotihuacán civilization consisted of more than 200,000 people. Numerous structures from this era still stand. The most prominent of these are the Pyramid of the Sun and the Pyramid of the Moon. Although no one knows why, this civilization came to an end around 700 CE. Meaning "birthplace of the gods," the name Teotihuacán was given to this abandoned city hundreds of years later by the Aztecs. The Teotihuacán ruins make up the most visited archaeological sites in all of Mexico.

The Maya

When many people think of ancient Mexican civilizations, the Mayan civilization is the first one that comes to mind. The Maya lived in the area that is now southern Mexico and Central America around 200 to 800 CE. They are credited with many advances in mathematics and astronomy, including the most accurate calendar ever created by that point in time. They also developed their own hieroglyphic writing that included names for gods and animals.

Like other ancient peoples, the Maya left behind numerous structures that lie in ruins today. Of these the most popular is Chichén Itzá, which is home to El Castillo, one of the best preserved pyramids still in existence. Mayan people still live in this area. These indigenous Mexicans continue to speak the language and practice many customs of their ancestors.

The Toltecs

The Toltec civilation flourished around 900 CE and continued until about 1200 CE. Although theirs was a short-lived civilization, the Toltecs are known for being talented artists, builders, and warriors. They are credited with being one of the first civilizations to use metals such as gold and copper in their sculptures.

The Toltecs' biggest downfall was their disagreement over religion. About half the Toltecs followed a warlike god, while the other half believed in a peaceful god. This division left the Toltecs weak when other tribes moved into the area and attacked them.

Atlantes statue at the Toltec Temple of the Morning Star (Venus), Tula, Mexico

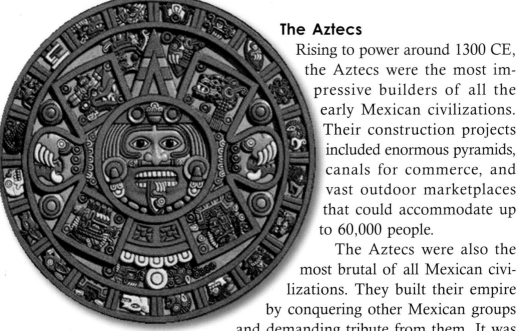

Center of the Sun Stone, painted by R. S. Flandes, 1939

The Aztecs

Rising to power around 1300 CE, the Aztecs were the most impressive builders of all the early Mexican civilizations. Their construction projects included enormous pyramids, canals for commerce, and vast outdoor marketplaces that could accommodate up to 60,000 people.

The Aztecs were also the most brutal of all Mexican civilizations. They built their empire by conquering other Mexican groups and demanding tribute from them. It was their human sacrifices, however, that set them far apart from other civilizations. Whereas the ancient Maya would make offerings of food to their gods, the Aztecs asked their gods for rain for their crops and victory in their battles in exchange for human hearts. In front of statues of their gods, they would cut the beating heart from the body of their sacrificial victim.

Spanish Conquest

In 1519, Spanish soldiers arrived in Mexico with the purpose of conquering the Aztecs, converting the remaining people to Catholicism, and finding gold. These soldiers were led by a man named Hernán Cortés. It took only two years for Cortés and his army to defeat the Aztecs. This may have been because the Spaniards outnumbered the Aztecs, or it might have been because many other indigenous people joined the side of Spain. During their rise to power, the Aztecs had made many enemies by taxing the people they had defeated.

The Spaniards bestowed their new land with the name New Spain in 1521. With this new era came Mexico City, Guadalajara, and other new cities, as well as new architecture. European-style buildings were constructed with Mexican materials, creating a pleasing blend of cultures. A great number of these new buildings—as many as 12,000—were churches. Although they had little choice in the matter, the Mexican people embraced Catholicism quite readily.

New Spain continued for the next 300 years. During this time the Spaniards found the gold they had been seeking—and silver, too. They used the indigenous people to mine these precious metals for them, treating them like slaves. Eventually, the Mexican people tired of their treatment by Spain. In 1810, rallied by a priest named Miguel Hidalgo, the Mexican people began to fight for their independence. The War of Independence was not an easy one. It lasted eleven years, but eventually Mexico emerged victorious.

The Nation of Mexico

The years that followed Mexico's victory in the War of Independence were filled with military rebellions, war with the United States over land, and even civil war. Mexico soon learned that self-government was a complicated undertaking.

Between 1863 and 1867, French troops occupied the country of Mexico. This act was overturned by one of Mexico's most celebrated presidents, Benito Juárez. Many historians refer to Juárez as Mexico's Abraham Lincoln. The two men presided over their countries during the same period in history, both served their terms during a time of war, and both showed great perseverance even in the face of initial defeat.

Today Mexico no longer has to fight to keep its land or go to war against other countries looking to enslave its people. It does, however, struggle with issues relating to its economy, governmental corruption, and the illegal drug trade. These are the problems that will define the country in the twenty-first century.

The various groups of Mayan people spoke about 30 closely related languages. These included Mayan and Huastec. Their written language consisted of over 800 distinct hieroglyphs.

FYI FACT

The once endangered gray whale occupies the warm-water lagoons of Baja California during winter. Unfortunately, the peninsula offers only a few protected areas where mothers can give birth to and care for their young before returning north.

Mexico's Natural Wonders

Mexico is the fifth-largest country in the Western Hemisphere. It covers 758,446 square miles (1,964,735 square kilometers). This is about three times the size of Texas. Only Canada, the United States, Brazil, and Argentina are larger than Mexico. No other country, though, offers the unique landscape that Mexico does. The geography of Mexico is filled with stunning contrasts. From bottomless canyons and towering mountains to lush wetlands and arid deserts, the Mexican wilderness is both welcoming and dangerous.

The country of Mexico is long and roughly triangular, tapering toward its southern border, which abuts Belize and Guatemala. Two enormous mountain ranges run along Mexico's east and west coasts. The Sierra Madre Oriental is situated along the eastern shoreline, and the Sierra Madre Occidental is located on the western seashore. The words *oriental* and *occidental* actually mean "east" and "west," respectively. Mexico also has prominent peninsulas—Baja California and the Yucatán. Baja California extends south from the border of the U.S. state of California. The Yucatán Peninsula, on the eastern side of Mexico, is home to Cancún, the most popular tourist destination in the country.

Its east coast is defined by the Gulf of Mexico, a large basin of the Atlantic Ocean. The gulf's warm waters draw a multitude of tourists to Mexico's sandy beaches. This body of water also provides a rich fishing resource for the Mexican people. Various types of fish, oysters, shrimp, and squid are plentiful in this area. Mexico's west coast, which

Puerto Vallarta is especially scenic. In addition to the natural beauty of its coastline, the area is known for its cobblestoned streets, red-tiled roofs, and windows edged with curling wrought iron.

spans approximately 2,000 miles (3,200 kilometers), is shaped by the Pacific Ocean. This area is often referred to as the Mexican Riviera. Including such popular vacation destinations as Puerto Vallarta and Acapulco, the west coast offers its visitors sandy beaches and mild winter weather.

The center section of the country is called the Plateau of Mexico. This is where the majority of Mexican people have always lived. When you hear the word *plateau,* you may imagine a flat, elevated piece of land, but the Plateau of Mexico differs greatly from this conventional image. While much of this land is indeed elevated, there is a surprising amount of diversity in this interior terrain. There you will also find hills, mountains, and even volcanoes. Measuring approximately 18,700 feet (5,700 meters), the country's highest peak is in fact one such volcano called Volcan Pico de Orizaba. Although the last eruption of this volcano occurred in 1687, Volcan Pico de Orizaba is classified as dormant, not extinct. Another volcano located on the Plateau of Mexico is called Ixtaccíhuatl. This volcano is considered essentially dormant, but it does release steam and smoke occasionally. Mexico's lowest elevation is located in the Mexicali Valley, which sits at approximately 32 feet (10 meters) below sea level.

With this varied terrain, Mexico also has a highly diverse climate. Instead of being warmest in the south, like many other North American countries, Mexico's hottest temperatures and most of its humid weather can be found at its lowest elevations, primarily on the coast. This area is called Tierra Caliente, which means "hot land." The Plateau of Mexico has milder temperatures, but the lack of humidity there can also pose problems. Because this area is home to the country's richest farmland, it is imperative that the rainy season indeed produce water for the thirsty crops. From May until October, it isn't unusual to see entire Mexican farming villages in their fields, praying for rain. Perhaps some of them are praying to Tlaloc, the ancient Aztec god of rain.

When you think of the vegetation in Mexico, the first plant that springs to mind is probably a cactus. Certainly, many types of cacti can be found in the deserts, but these are hardly the only plants that prosper in Mexico. The country's tropical areas produce many delicate flowers and delicious fruits. Dahlia pinnatas and orchids grow wild in southern sections of Mexico, particularly after heavy rains. Bananas, grapefruits, mangoes, oranges, and papayas can also be found there.

Because of the various types of terrain and temperatures, a large assortment of animals lives in Mexico. In the deserts one can find armadillos, rabbits, and snakes. More exotic species like jaguars, monkeys, and parrots live in the Mexican rain forests. In the mountains there are animals more similar to those found in the rest of North America—including coyotes and pumas. Unfortunately, numbers of many of these species are declining. Highways have given hunters unlimited access to wildlife that once resided in the most remote areas of the country. Farmers too have caused the downfall of many species, by moving onto the land once occupied by these animals.

Tierra Caliente is also a type of music that combines fiddles, guitars, and harps. Lyrics tell romantic or funny stories.

FYI FACT

A woman buys flowers from an outdoor merchant in Cuetzalan, a mountainous town in the state of Puebla. The people there have preserved many Aztec traditions and customs.

The People of Mexico

The troubled history of Mexico plays a large role in its people's heritage. The majority of Mexicans have both indigenous and European blood in their ancestry, a result of the wars and conquests that have taken place on their country's soil. People of this mixed heritage are called mestizos. Amerindians, or indigenous people, and whites (*güeros*) also live in Mexico, but it is hard to say for certain how much of each race makes up the Mexican population. No census has kept track of this information for nearly a century. The government estimates that 60 percent of the Mexican population is mestizo, 30 percent are Amerindian, and 10 percent are either *güeros* or other races.

Anyone in Mexico can choose to live an indigenous life, which many Mexican people describe as being more about a lifestyle choice than a bloodline. *Indígenas,* the name used for both indigenous people and those who adopt their lifestyle, usually live in very specific regions, such as the state of Chiapas, which is located near the border with Guatemala. Some people view the *indígenas* as a separate society. *Indígenas* practice what is thought of as the old ways. They live off the land, and they believe in traditional values.

Religious faith is a huge part of most Mexicans' lives. Nearly 80 percent of all Mexican people are Catholic. One of the biggest differences between the *indígenas* and the mestizos, though, is that the *indígenas* blend ancient religious customs with Catholicism. It is not unusual to see *indígenas* praying to statues of Catholic saints before

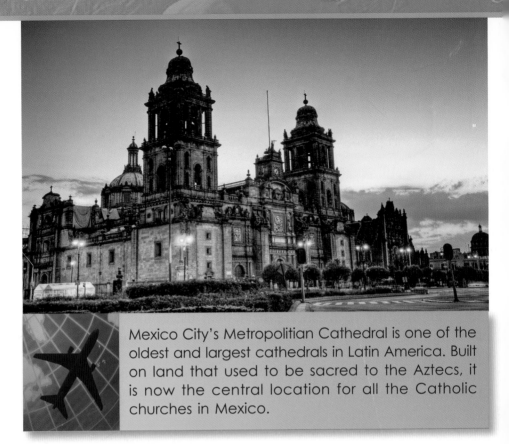

Mexico City's Metropolitian Cathedral is one of the oldest and largest cathedrals in Latin America. Built on land that used to be sacred to the Aztecs, it is now the central location for all the Catholic churches in Mexico.

leaving gifts such as food at the statues' feet. The practice of leaving gifts at statues of gods is part of the Mayan religion.

The children growing up in Mexico around 2010 have greater opportunities for education than any generation before them. At the time of the Mexican Revolution (1910–1920), only 15 percent of the Mexican population could read and write. Soon afterwards, though, the Mexican government made building a public school system a priority. For many decades this developing system did not reach into rural areas. A century later, however, children of all walks of life in Mexico have the opportunity to attend school.

At the age of six, Mexican children begin primary school, which spans grades one through six. Grades seven, eight, and nine are grouped together as secondary school, this country's version of middle school. The Mexican equivalent of high school is called preparatory school, and it lasts for three more years. Upon graduating from preparatory school, a student may then decide to apply to a university for a college education.

One of the ways that Mexico is trying to reverse its significant dropout rate is by putting teachers out on the streets—literally. In some cities teachers hold classes outdoors, wherever they can create a make-shift classroom. The hope is that by reaching out to these kids, teachers may be able to inspire them to finish their education.

With the Mexican population well over 100 million and growing, keeping kids in school can only make life better for the Mexican people. The majority of the Mexican people live in urban areas. As much as a quarter of the Mexican population lives in Mexico City alone. With an education, there is hope for prosperity.

Even with all the day-to-day struggles many people face, most Mexicans are proud of their heritage. In addition to the more universal holidays celebrated in other countries, such as New Year's Day and

A class tries on newly donated sports jerseys.

Cinco de Mayo celebrations, which symbolize unity, include traditional music, food, and clothing.

Christmas, Mexico has many important holidays of its own. Most center on the country's rich history.

Although people in many other countries love to celebrate the Mexican holiday of Cinco de Mayo, many do not know what it is they are celebrating. Spanish for "the Fifth of May," Cinco de Mayo marks the anniversary of the 1862 Battle of Puebla. This battle was won by a small troop of Mexican soldiers against a much larger and more experienced French army. The victory is now a symbol of both the patriotism and perseverance of the Mexican people. Cinco de Mayo celebrations often include military parades and speeches by politicians, as well as lots of food and other festivities.

FYI FACT:

Many Mexican people share their homes with extended family members. It is very common for Mexican children to grow up under the same roof as their grandparents, aunts, uncles, and cousins.

Some people confuse Cinco de Mayo with Mexico's Independence Day, but the two are completely different holidays. Independence Day, known in Mexico as El Grito de Independencia, is celebrated every year on September 16. On the eve of this important date in 1810, Miguel Hidalgo made a very famous speech called El Grito de Dolores. Although no one knows the exact words Hidalgo used, the speech is still considered the call to action that ultimately unified the Mexican people to win their independence from Spain in 1821.

Independence Day is a time of great celebration for the Mexican people. Like Cinco de Mayo, it inspires extreme feelings of pride and patriotism. Each year on the eve of Independence Day, fireworks are launched, the country's national anthem is played, and the people shout, *"Viva Hidalgo! Viva independencia! Viva Mexico!"* The holiday itself is usually marked with parades and more patriotic music.

Another popular Mexican holiday is Días de los Muertos. Despite meaning "days of the dead," Días de los Muertos is actually a celebration of both the living and the dead. It also spans three days. On the last day of October each year, Mexican people begin preparations to honor family and friends who have passed. On the first and second days of November, they celebrate the lives of these lost loved ones. The spirits of these individuals are believed to return to the earth for just one day—children on the 1st and adults on the 2nd.

On Días de los Muertos, people decorate the graves of their lost family members and friends with fresh flowers. They also make lots of food and create papier-mâché sculptures of whimsical skeletons that they place on altars. They then play lively music, eat delicious food, and honor both the life and the death of people close to them who have died.

FYI FACT:

One of the oldest inhabitants of Mexico is the Chihuahua. The ancestors of this tiny dog breed can be traced back to the Toltec civilization. Today's Chihuahuas are named after the Mexican state of Chihuahua.

Hugo Sánchez played for Mexico in the 1993 World Cup qualifying match against Honduras.

Mexican Culture

In colonial times, the most popular spectator sport in Mexico was bullfighting. Today, however, the biggest pastime of the country is *fútbol,* the sport known in the United States as soccer. In Mexico, people enjoy watching *fútbol* both in person and on television. They also enjoy playing the sport. Many kids play on *fútbol* teams at school, and people everywhere kick balls around or play pickup games whenever and wherever they can.

Although Mexico hasn't won as many World Cups as fellow *fútbol-*crazed countries Argentina and Brazil, Mexico has its fair share of famous players in its history. Manuel Sánchez played in the very first World Cup competition in 1930. He was also the first player to score a goal from a penalty kick at the World Cup level. As an added bonus to his country, this goal was against one of Mexico's biggest rivals, Argentina.

Hugo Sánchez is known not only in his home country of Mexico, but also in Europe. He was in fact the first Mexican player to make a name for himself overseas. He scored 234 goals in his impressive career. Now retired, he is a coach for his home country. Luis Hernández and Rafael Marquez also earned their places in Mexican *fútbol* history by being high scorers. Hernández was twice named Mexican Player of the Year, and Marquez was known for being one of the most adaptable defense players ever, effortlessly moving among the positions of center back, defensive midfielder, and even left or right back.

Other sports are also popular in Mexico. The Mexican people began playing *béisbol* (baseball) in the early 1900s. Over the years the country has sent many players to play on professional teams in the United States. Bobby Ávila was the first such player to make it big in the U.S. Born in Veracruz, Mexico, he joined the Cleveland Indians in 1949. During his career as second baseman, he also played for the Baltimore Orioles, the Boston Red Sox, and the Milwaukee Braves. After retiring as a player, Ávila returned to Mexico and became the president of the Mexican League.

Though popular throughout Mexico, basketball is played primarily in the cities. Outdoor courts can be found in almost any city park, making it easy for virtually anyone to play. American-style football, or *fútbol Americano,* is becoming more popular in Mexico, but it is unlikely to draw the same number of players as other sports anytime soon. The equipment that players must wear to play the game is expensive. Mexican schools can afford to buy soccer balls much more easily than all the helmets and pads needed to play this less popular sport.

Although bullfighting is no longer the top sport of Mexico, it is still a mighty popular pastime for many Mexican people. Thousands of bullfights still take place in Mexico each year. A bullring in Mexico City called Plaza México is the largest stadium of its kind in the world. It can hold up to 50,000 spectators. Plaza México holds a special bullfight each February called the Corrida de Aniversario. This special event has been held every year since the stadium was built in 1946.

At the beginning of a bullfighting event, a trumpet or band music is played. Usually there is also a parade. The purpose of this opening ceremony is to get the crowd excited for the fight that will follow. The human competitor in a bullfighting contest is called a matador. Matadors put on an elaborate show for the people who come to see bullfights. They dress in decorative costumes and display enormous courage when the bulls charge them, one at a time. Most bullfighters hold a red cape to get the attention of the bulls. The color red is said to make bulls angry.

Each time the bull charges the matador, the animal's pointed horns come dangerously close to impaling the human contender. Often just

FYI FACT:

The largest bullfighting arena is the Plaza de Toros México in central Mexico City. It seats 48,000 people.

The Palace of Fine Arts,
Mexico City

a few inches denote the difference between life and death. As the matador pulls the cape out of the way at the last second, the crowd shouts, "Ole!" This Spanish exclamation is used to express appreciation of the matador's performance. The matador shows no fear, even though the bulls are bred to be as mean and ornery as possible.

Many people feel bullfighting is a cruel sport. At the end of each bullfight, the matador kills the bull by thrusting a sword into the back of its neck. Many animal rights groups think that bullfighting is a sport that should be left in the past. Others feel that bullfighting is an important part of Mexican tradition. These two groups are unlikely to find common ground about this controversial issue.

The Mexican people also enjoy a variety of performing arts. A large concert hall called the Palace of Fine Arts (Palacio de Bellas Artes) is located in Mexico City's downtown area. It hosts a variety of performances—such as ballet, opera, and plays. The galleries of the hall display many prized murals by such artists as Diego Rivera, David Alfaro Siqueiros, and José Clemente Orozco.

Students from all over the country flock to Mexico City to study various performing arts. The National Center for the Arts opened in 1994. It offers classes in art, dance, music, and theater.

When they aren't watching *fútbol* games or enjoying the arts, the Mexican people enjoy spending time at home with their families. Each day in the mid-afternoon, the people take a break called a siesta. During this time, shops and offices shut down. They reopen later in the day after everyone has had the opportunity for a short nap and an afternoon meal with loved ones. Many people in the United States find this practice unusual, but the Mexican people regard the siesta as one of their most treasured customs.

FYI FACT:

Mexican music is often played by mariachi bands. These traditional performers play such instruments as acoustic guitars, trumpets, and violins. The mariachis' colorful outfits, called charro suits, are topped off with wide-brimmed hats called sombreros.

If you visit Mexico, you may find a Walmart, but the produce it sells—including cacti—may differ somewhat from what you find at your local store.

The Mexican Economy

Most Mexican people struggle to make ends meet. The single largest private employer in the country is Walmart, the US-owned chain known around the world for its low prices. More than 100,000 Mexican people work for Walmart. With more than 1 million people reaching working age in Mexico each year, though, competition for these jobs is fierce.

Other jobs in the service industry, like teaching schoolchildren or working at a bank as an accountant, require more education than jobs as store clerks do. The best-paying jobs in Mexico are those in the field of computer science and technology, but these too usually require post-secondary education. With about half the population dropping out of school before the age of fourteen, this leaves many young Mexicans without much hope for a good-paying job.

While Walmart is Mexico's largest private employer, the company is not the country's biggest moneymaker. Making billions of dollars every year, the petroleum industry makes Mexico the leading oil producer in all of Latin America. The majority of this oil is exported to the United States. Unfortunately, this does not translate to a large number of jobs for Mexican people. Mining metals such as silver also does not provide the number of jobs that one might think. Over 2 million metric tons of silver is mined in Mexico every year, but more and more metals are being extracted by machinery.

In bigger cities like Monterrey, numerous types of factories provide steady work for thousands of Mexicans. These people are the lucky ones, even though many Mexican factory workers make the same wage in a day that a similar U.S. worker makes in one hour. Factories may produce automobiles and vehicle parts, clothing and shoes, computers, concrete and steel, or even soft drinks. There are not enough factory jobs for everyone. Many international companies that used to contract work to Mexico have moved their factories from Mexico to countries such as China and India, where they can pay their workers even less.

Many city dwellers without steady jobs are forced to make their living more sporadically. Some of these people offer ordinary services like shoe shining and car window washing in the streets. Others perform dangerous stunts like fire-eating in hopes of earning some pocket change from the gaping crowds. Street performers like musicians and magicians can also be found on the streets of many cities.

In more rural areas, many Mexican people earn their living by farming, but rocky soil and infrequent rain make growing crops diffi-

Dried corn husks are commonly used to wrap fresh corn tamales, a traditional Mexican dish. Corn husks are also used in numerous Mexican crafts.

FYI FACT:

The jicama (HEE-kuh-muh), or Mexican potato, is widely grown in Mexico. It looks like a turnip but tastes like a cross between a pear and an apple. People eat it raw or cooked. To make a refreshing snack, peel and slice some raw jicama, then drizzle it with lemon juice and sprinkle with salt.

cult, if not impossible, in many areas. Only about 12 percent of the total land in Mexico is suitable for farming. The best location for growing crops is the southern half of the Plateau of Mexico. This is where much of the country's corn is grown. Corn is an important crop, because it is used to make tortillas, the staple Mexican bread used in a number of popular Mexican dishes. More than half of Mexican farmland is dedicated to growing corn. Other crops that are commonly grown include bananas, cotton, and a variety of citrus fruits such as lemons and oranges.

People who live on the Mexican coasts often make their living in the hospitality industry. Millions of people visit Mexico each year, spending billions of dollars while on vacation there. Hotels and restaurants make tourism a promising enterprise for those who own land in the warm areas along the coast.

The biggest stumbling block to a stable economy throughout Mexico is overpopulation. More than 20 million people live in Mexico City alone. By 2040, this number is expected to triple. Because the Mexican population is growing so rapidly, the unemployment rate is staggering. This number is even worse than collected data shows. The many people who work a day here and a day there on the streets of Mexico are not counted as part of the population without jobs.

Mexico has free-trade agreements with over 50 countries—including El Salvador, Guatemala, Honduras, the European Free Trade Area, and Japan.

FYI FACT

A giant sculpture of the head of former Mexican president Lázaro Cárdenas sits in Guerrero. Cárdenas is known for nationalizing the country's oil.

Mexican Government

The official name of the country of Mexico is Los Estados Unidos Mexicanos, which means the United Mexican States. Although this name sounds a lot like the United States of America, the way the government works in Mexico is somewhat different from how it works in the U.S. From the outside the two systems look remarkably similar, but a closer look reveals some striking differences.

Thirty-one states and one federal district make up Los Estados Unidos Mexicanos. This federal district encompasses Mexico City and some of its surroundings. Each state has a governor who is elected by the Mexican people. Every Mexican citizen over the age of eighteen has the right to vote in both local and federal elections. The federal government, however, can replace or suspend any leader if it deems it necessary.

As it is in the United States, the federal government of Mexico is divided into three branches: the executive branch, the legislative branch, and the judicial branch. The president is in charge of the executive branch. In addition to commanding the country's armed forces, the president is also responsible for appointing a cabinet, the group of people who help the president run the various sections of the government. This too is very similar to how things are run in the United States. Whereas an American president is elected to a four-year term, however, a Mexican president is elected for six years, and he or she cannot run for a second term. There is also no vice president. If any-

Mexican President Vicente Fox (2000–2006) speaks before the Mexican Congress in his fourth State of the Union address.

thing keeps the president from finishing his or her term in office, the legislative branch appoints a replacement.

For over seventy years, the Mexican presidency was held by a member of the PRI party, which stands for Partido Revolucionario Institucional, or Institutional Revolutionary Party. In the year 2000, Vicente Fox did what no other politician had been able to do since 1929: He managed to win the presidential election without belonging to the PRI. Fox's campaign platform was based largely on his pledge to clean up corruption. Although Fox left office in 2006, many Mexican people still see his election as a turning point in Mexico's history. He was succeeded by Felipe Calderón.

The legislative branch of Mexico's government is called Congreso de la Union (Congress of the Union). This two-part branch is responsible for making the country's laws. The Mexican Senate is made up of 128 members, and the Chamber of Deputies is made up of 500 members. Like the president, senators are elected to a single six-year term. Deputies, on the other hand, are elected to three-year terms. They are allowed to run again, but they cannot be elected to two terms in a row.

Mexico's judicial branch is headed by the Supreme Court of Justice. It is made up of 21 members. Like the U.S. Supreme Court, these members are appointed by the president and confirmed (or approved) by the Senate. Circuit courts and district courts also help interpret local and federal laws.

The greatest difference between the governments of the United States and Mexico is how government officials enforce the law. For some legal infractions, such as speeding while driving, Mexican police may accept bribes called *mordidas* instead of summonsing offenders to court. Although there is no written explanation or record of *mordidas,* nearly all Mexican people have come to know about this corrupt system. Even utility workers and sanitation workers have begun to utilize *mordidas* as a means of supplementing their income, and the people have learned that paying these bribes is the quickest way to get necessary services such as swift telephone repair and garbage collection.

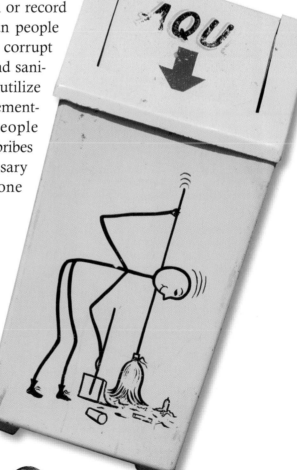

Garbage can in Puerto Vallarta

Griselda Álvarez, the first female governor of a Mexican state, believed education was the way to progress.

Famous People of Mexico

Many Mexican people are known throughout their native land. Some are even famous well beyond the borders of Mexico.

Griselda Álvarez

Griselda Álvarez is known for being the first female governor of a Mexican state. Born on April 5, 1913, in Guadalajara, Jalisco, Álvarez once said that politics was in her blood and lifeline. She claimed that even as a child, she knew that either she or her sister would grow up to become a governor of Colima. In 1857, Álvarez's great-grandfather, Manuel Álvarez, became the first governor of the state. Her father, Miguel Álvarez, also served as governor of the state from 1919 to 1923.

Her early ambitions didn't seem to be in line with politics. Álvarez received a degree in writing and composition from the National Autonomous University of Mexico. Then, while writing both poetry and prose, she worked as a teacher before moving on to work under the secretary of education. From 1976 to 1979, she served as a senator for the state of Jalisco. The role for which Álvarez will forever be known, however, began in 1979 when she was elected Governor of Colima as her father and grandfather had been before her.

Álvarez's term as governor expired in 1985, but her accomplishments didn't end there. She went on to found several important organizations such as the Center of Attention to Women and the Mexican Women's Alliance. She died in Mexico City in 2009.

Guillermo González Camarena

If you have spent any time watching television recently, you have a Mexican man named Guillermo González Camarena to thank for it. Camarena is known throughout the world for being the inventor of color television. Born in 1917 in Guadalajara, Camarena was a prolific child. At the age of twelve, he had already built his first amateur radio. By seventeen he had built his own television camera.

He graduated from the School of Mechanical and Electrical Engineers at the National Polytechnic Institute in Mexico City in 1930. Like Álvarez, Camarena went on to work in education. After graduation he took a job as an operator at the radio station of Mexico's Department of Public Education.

His defining accomplishment began when he created a piece of equipment called a trichromatic adapter. The device made it possible for color images to be transmitted by wire. This groundbreaking invention was then used to upgrade black-and-white television transmission to a color system. Camarena broadcast the first color image from his lab at the Mexican League of Radio Experiments in

1946. The first official color broadcast in Mexico took place in 1963 on a station that Camarena had established in 1952.

Camarena was killed in a car accident in 1965. He was on his way home from inspecting a television transmitter in Las Lajas, Veracruz. In 1995, the Guillermo González Camarena Foundation (La Fundación Guillermo González Camarena) was formed. This organization helps to nurture the talent and creativity of other Mexican inventors.

César Chávez

César Chávez is known throughout the world as being an advocate of Mexican immigrants in the United States. Many Mexican people who come to the United States find work on farms in the southwestern areas of the country. Called migrant farm workers, they move from farm to farm as work becomes available in different areas. This difficult work does not pay well. It can also be dangerous—for example, workers come into contact with pesticides that are used on many of the crops. Chávez made it his life's work to fight for the rights of these migrant workers.

The grandson of a Mexican immigrant, Chávez was no stranger to working on a farm. He was born in 1927 in San Luis, Arizona, where his parents owned a farm. When he was ten years old, though, his family lost their farm as a result of the Great Depression, a grueling economic time for many people in the United States. Chávez and his family were forced to find jobs as migrant farm workers to support themselves at this time.

FYI FACT:

In 2003, the United States Postal Service unveiled a stamp to honor the life and work of César Chávez.

As an adult Chávez began rallying to improve working conditions and safety for migrant farm workers. He also worked to increase wages to a more reasonable amount. He helped organize *huelgas* (strikes) and boycotts of foods grown by farms that refused to offer safer working conditions and better pay. In 1962, he helped found a union for migrant farm workers called the National Farm Workers Association (NFWA). In 1966, when the organization merged with a Filipino American group called the Agricultural Workers Organizing Committee (AWOC), the name was changed to the United Farm Workers (UFW).

Although he died in 1993, Chávez is still celebrated as a champion of Mexican-American people. In 1994 he was posthumously awarded the Presidential Medal of Freedom. The UFW and Chávez's children and grandchildren have continued his work to protect the rights of migrant farm workers.

Octavio Paz

Octavio Paz began his life in 1914 in Mexico City, but his eighty-four years took him all over the world. Exposed to books at an early age, Paz seemed destined to become a writer. Both his father and grandfather were political journalists. Octavio published his first book of poems before he was twenty. Just a few years later, he helped found a literary magazine called *Taller.* During this time his work took him to Spain and the United States.

In 1945 Paz decided to add diplomatic service to his resume. He was sent to France, where he continued his writing along with this new political work. He also served as ambassador to France, Switzerland, and Japan. He was appointed ambassador to India in 1962. He resigned just six years later, though. He did this out of protest when Mexican security forces killed hundreds of student demonstrators in Mexico City at the time of the Olympic Games.

Paz wrote both poetry and prose throughout his life, and had more than 40 books published. In 1990 he made history when he became the first Mexican writer to win the highest literary award, the Nobel Prize for literature. In 1998, Paz died in the same city where he was born.

Thalía

Many people of Mexican descent have made it big in the United States. Some can be heard singing on the radio. Others can be seen acting on television or in movies. Still others have become famous for their dancing abilities. The most popular singer, actress, and dancer in Mexico, though, are the same person. Her name is Thalía.

Born Ariadna Thalía Sodi Miranda in 1971, this talented artist has been performing since she was a youngster. As a child, she was a member of the singing groups Din Din and Timbiriche. As a teenager, Thalía was given the opportunity to be part of *Quinceañera,* the first television soap opera for teens.

It wasn't until the 1990s, though, that Thalía's career really took off. She continued both singing and acting during this time. She is now known throughout her native land and in many other countries as well. She has sold more than 20 million albums worldwide.

Dancers perform in Guadalajara. The costumes used in most Mexican festivals are extremely colorful. The vibrant hues are an excellent match for the passionate Mexican dancers who wear them.

Chapter

9

Mexican Festivals

One of the best things about many of the people of Mexico is their remarkable ability to appreciate the present moment. Even through times of economic hardship, a large part of Mexican culture involves vibrant celebrations, sometimes called fiestas. Mexican festivals engage all of the partygoers' senses. Brightly colored clothes, upbeat music, and delicious food are a part of nearly every Mexican fiesta. Whatever the country lacks in terms of material riches, its glorious people make up for in their ability to see the glass as half full—and in their willingness to share that glass with others.

The best known Mexican festival is called Carnival, or Carnaval (pronounced kar-nih-VAL). This weeklong celebration beginning in February or March is said to be an opportunity for people to get all the craziness out of their systems before the more serious period of Lent. Lent, which begins on Ash Wednesday and ends at Easter, is an annual season of fasting and self-reflection for Roman Catholics. Carnival is celebrated throughout the world, but it is especially popular in Mexico.

Carnival celebrations in Mexico typically involve parades and street performances, day and night. Many Mexican towns even set up fair-type games and amusement rides. People wear wild costumes, dance to live music, and eat festive foods. Both clothing and food tend to relate to the surrounding areas in some way. Costume contests are held, and kings and queens of parades are named. People often say that celebrating Carnival is so exhausting that they feel like they need a vacation from their vacation when it's over.

Another popular Mexican festival called Guelaguetza occurs during the last two weeks of July each year. As is the case with Carnival, visitors from around the world attend this festival, which takes place in Oaxaca (whah-HAH-kuh), the city of the state of the same name in the southeastern part of country. In celebration of Guelaguetza, dancers from around the state gather at an outdoor amphitheater and perform on the last two Mondays of the month as an expression of their culture.

The word *Guelaguetza* means "shared offering." The dance performances are considered an offering to the ancient Mexican gods in exchange for rain and a bountiful harvest. When the performances conclude, though, there is another, more tangible offering. The performers actually throw gifts from the stage to audience members.

An annual dance festival called Guelaguetza takes place every year in Oaxaca. The event honors several indigenous gods, including Centeotl, the Zapotec and Miztec goddess of corn.

Every October since 1972, the Mexican people have gathered in Guanajuato, Mexico, to honor the life and works of Miguel de Cervantes, the Spanish author, poet, and playwright who lived from 1547 to 1616. Many people regard Cervantes' book *Don Quixote* as one of the best novels ever written. The Festival Internacional Cervantino draws an international audience. Each year a different country and a Mexican state are given the spotlight with a focus on cultural performances from these regions. Performances may range from art exhibitions to dance to theatrical shows. This custom-made theme makes the festival a completely different event each time it occurs.

The Yucatán Bird Festival is a much younger event. Beginning in 2002, it has quickly become a very popular celebration for bird-watchers everywhere. It takes place in the state of Yucatán, a highly popular destination in its own right. Timing a vacation to coincide with this late-fall celebration can make a trip to Mexico even more fun. An experienced bird-watcher may even bring home a trophy as a souvenir.

One of the biggest attractions of the Yucatán Bird Festival is something called Xoc ch'ich (show CHEE-eech), which means "count bird" in the Mayan language. Teams of up to eight people each compete to find the most bird species they can within the three-day period. With more than 400 bird species registered in Yucatán, even the professional guide who leads each team may spot something new during the contest.

In addition to the Xoc ch'ich, the Yucatán Bird Festival also features guest speakers, workshops, and tours. Bird-watchers from both near and far can meet and discuss their favorite subject: birds. Some events are held for children who are just beginning to learn about this pastime.

FYI FACT:

Many Mexican festivals include piñatas. These fun party decorations contain loads of wrapped candy. Partygoers wear blindfolds as they take turns swinging a stick at the piñata. When the package breaks, all the goodies from the inside fall to the ground, where the children can grab handfuls at a time.

The island of Cozumel is filled with numerous Mayan ruin sites, including Tulum.

We Visit Mexico

If you plan to visit Mexico, make a point of adding the following areas and attractions to your schedule.

Cozumel

The island of Cozumel is located just off the coast of Cancún on the Yucatán Peninsula. If you are staying in Cancún, Cozumel is just a short ferry ride away. Although a fair portion of the island has sprouted hotels and restaurants for tourists, much of the island sports numerous Mayan ruins. These include San Gervasio and El Cedral.

In ancient times, San Gervasio was a sacred place for the women. Every Mayan woman was expected to travel from the mainland to Cozumel at least once in her lifetime. The purpose of the trip was to make offerings to Ixchel, the goddess of fertility and rain. It was believed that by doing so, she would be blessed with babies and bountiful crops at home.

El Cedral was the first Mexican site found by Spanish explorers in 1518. It is also believed to have been the location of the first Catholic mass in Mexico. Interestingly, El Cedral was used as a jail in the 1800s. In the present day, El Cedral is home to an annual fair called the Festival de Cedral. For several nights each May, tourists can enjoy music and dancing and even attend bullfights there.

Crested Caracara

Isla Mujeres

Isla Mujeres (Island of Women) is the easternmost point of Mexico. For this reason one of the best times to visit this Mexican island is New Year's Eve. Each year on this holiday, there is a tradition for everyone to greet the first rays of the New Year's sun together at dawn.

If you enjoy pirate stories, Isla Mujeres has many of them in its history. Such legendary pirates as Henry Morgan and Jean Lafitte are said to have spent time walking Mujeres' sandy beaches. It is also said that they left their women on the island to keep them safe while the men sailed the high seas. Some people even believe that these pirates buried some of their famous treasures on Isla Mujeres.

Monte Álban

Monte Álban is a fascinating hilltop archaeological site in the southern state of Oaxaca. Most famous for its underground tombs, Monte Álban also includes an ancient ball court, a massive stone staircase, and numerous other monuments. One structure at the site is believed to have served as an ancient astronomical observatory. A network of tunnels spreads out underneath the central plaza, connecting the various parts of the site.

Visitors can easily spend a couple of hours touring the site and wandering the underground passageways. Among the attractions are more than 170 tombs, numerous ceremonial altars, and even pyramids. There is also a wonderful site museum and a café that offers a breathtaking view of the Oaxaca Valley.

FYI FACT:

If you are planning to visit Mexico, you may be warned, "Don't drink the water!" Many Americans get sick from drinking Mexican tap water. You can avoid this problem by drinking only bottled water (and not using ice) while visiting the country.

Other popular ruins in Mexico include Teotihuacán, Chichén Itzá, and Tulum.

Sumidero Canyon

Located in the state of Chiapas, Sumidero Canyon is one of the most beautiful natural wonders of Mexico. The canyon walls rise as high as 2,500 feet (750 meters), and the riverbed plunges as deep as 330 feet (100 meters). A boat tour through the canyon can take two to three hours, but the views are spectacular.

The canyon was formed by the Río Grijalva. At one time this river flowed freely through the canyon and was not even navigable. In 1981, though, the Chicoasen Hydroelectric Dam opened. Making water levels rise, the dam turned the river into a much calmer and safer place for boating.

One especially popular section of the canyon has been named Christmas Tree Falls. Green moss covers the tiers of rocks in this area. The structure looks like the boughs of a Christmas tree.

Visitors can mountain bike, hike, kayak, and swim in a nearby ecological park. Numerous species of wildlife inhabit the surrounding area. These include herons, egrets, kingfishers, and even monkeys. The park is also home to a wildlife sanctuary.

Pan Dulce

Mexico is known for its spicy main dishes, but did you know that many of Mexico's best culinary treasures are its desserts? *Pan dulce* is a delicious Mexican sweet bread. There are said to be more than 1,000 varieties, each one a favorite of somebody.

Ingredients:
1 loaf frozen bread dough
½ cup sugar
½ cup flour
¼ cup melted butter
1 large egg
½ teaspoon cinnamon

Directions:
1 Remove the bread dough from the freezer and let it thaw. Then cut it into about a dozen equal pieces. Next, roll each piece into a ball.
2 Place the balls on a greased cookie sheet, about 2 inches apart. Push down gently each ball with the palm of your hand until the top is flat.
3 Mix together the sugar, flour, butter, egg, and cinnamon. Brush some of the topping on each ball. Allow the rolls to rise until they have doubled in size.
4 Preheat the oven to 400°F. Under adult supervision, bake about 10 minutes, until the rolls are golden brown.
5 Remove from the pan immediately and cool on a wire rack. Makes 12 sweet rolls.

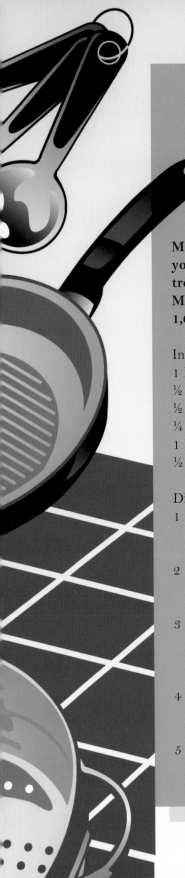

Cascarones

Cascarones **are a traditional craft that Mexican kids make at Easter and on other holidays. From the outside these decorated eggs look much like regular Easter eggs. Inside, though, cascarones are filled with confetti. For extra fun at holidays, kids make wishes before bumping the eggs on or over their friends' foreheads. If the egg breaks and the confetti spills out, it is said that the wish will come true.**

Materials:
1 dozen eggs
egg dying kit
confetti
tissue paper
glue

Instructions:
Gently tap on the pointed end of each egg until you make a small break in the shell. Then peel the shell back until you have created a hole about ½-inch in diameter. Empty the contents of the egg into a small bowl. (The whites and yolks can be whisked to make scrambled eggs for a family breakfast.) Rinse the egg under a gentle stream of water until it is completely empty. You may need to shake some of the water out. Let the eggs dry.

Following the directions on the egg dying kit, color the eggs. Once they are dry, finish decorating the outside, fill with confetti, and glue small pieces of tissue paper over the openings. You can find premade confetti at most party supply stores, or you can make your own with colored paper and a cross-cut paper shredder.

BCE

7000   Agriculture becomes a common way of life in Mexico, leaving time to develop industry, government, and religion

1200   Beginning of Olmec civilization

200   Beginning of Teotihuacán civilization

CE

200   Beginning of Mayan civilization

900   Beginning of Toltec civilization

1300   Beginning of Aztec civilization

1519   Spanish soldiers arrive in Mexico

1810   Miguel Hidalgo inspires Mexican people to fight for their independence

1821   Mexico wins its independence from Spain

1823   Mexico declares itself a federal republic

1863   Beginning of French occupation

1864   Federal republic ends; Second Mexican Empire begins

1910   Beginning of the Mexican Revolution, led by Emiliano Zapata

1916   U.S. forces pursue Pancho Villa into Mexico

1929   The National Revolutionary Party is formed; it will be renamed the PRI

1942   Mexico enters World War II by declaring war on Japan and Germany

1968   Hundreds of student demonstrators are massacred in Mexico City

1976   Huge deposits of oil are discovered offshore

1985   Devastating earthquake in Mexico City kills thousands

1993   Mexican government ratifies NAFTA with the United States and Canada

1995   The Mexican government agrees to give the indigenous Maya of Chiapas more autonomy

2000   Vicente Fox becomes first Mexican president in 71 years who is not a member of the PRI party

2006   In an effort to curb illegal immigration, U.S. President George W. Bush signs legislation to build a 700-mile- (1,125-kilometer-) long fence along the U.S.-Mexico border; Felipe Calderón becomes president of Mexico on December 1

2008   Mexico declares war on its drug cartels

2010   Mexico celebrates the Bicentennial of its Independence and the Centennial of the Mexican Revolution

Books

Perl, Lila. *People of the Ancient World: The Ancient Maya.* New York: Franklin
    Watts, 2005.

Saffer, Barbara. *Countries and Cultures—Mexico.* Mankato, Minnesota: Capstone
    Press, 2006.

Stein, R. Conrad. *Enchantment of the World—Mexico.* New York: Scholastic Library
    Publishing, 2007.

Streissguth, Tom. *Country Explorers—Mexico.* Minneapolis, Minnesota: Lerner
    Publications, 2008.

Works Consulted

American Kennel Club: Chihuahua History.
    http://www.akc.org/breeds/chihuahua/history

Baird, David. *Frommer's Mexico 2010.* Hoboken, New Jersey: Frommer's, 2009.

Baquedano, Elizabeth. *Aztec, Inca, and Maya.* New York: Alfred A. Knopf, 1993.

Franz, Carl. *The People's Guide to Mexico.* Emeryville, California: Avalon Travel
    Publishing, 2002.

Puig, Carlos. "The American Era Begins." *World Press Review,* January, 1994.

Rodriguez, Victoria Elizabeth. *Women in Contemporary Mexican Politics.* Austin:
    University of Texas Press, 2003.

Rule, Sheila. "Octavio Paz, Mexican Poet, Wins Nobel Prize." *New York Times,*
    October 12, 1990.

Sullivan, Kevin. "After Four Centuries, Silver Still Shines for Mexican Town."
    Washington Post, October 26, 2001.

UFW: Official Page of the United Farm Workers. http://www.ufw.org/

Vanderpool, Tim. "Cross-border Tensions Mount Over Bullfighting." *Christian
    Science Monitor,* December 8, 1999.

Wilkinson, Tracy. "Celebrating the First Mexican Astronaut: Out of This World!"
    Los Angeles Times, August 24, 2009.

On the Internet

CIA World Factbook: Mexico
    https://www.cia.gov/library/publications/the-world-factbook/geos/mx.html

Kids National Geographic
    http://kids.nationalgeographic.com/kids/places/find/mexico/

Mexico Para Ninos (in Spanish)
    http://www.elkiosco.gob.mx/

Time For Kids
    http://www.timeforkids.com/TFK/specials/goplaces/0,12405,176084,00.html

ambassador (am-BAS-uh-dor)—An official representative of a country who resides in another country while performing his or her diplomatic duties.

boycott (BOY-kot)—To refuse to buy a company's product as a way to protest the company's policies.

culture (KUL-cher)—The combination of beliefs, behaviors, traditions, and values shared by a particular group of people.

dormant (DOR-munt)—Of a volcano, inactive but still capable of erupting.

executive branch (ik-ZEK-yuh-tiv BRANCH)—The section of the government that includes the president and his cabinet.

export (EK-sport)—To ship goods out of the country for sale.

hieroglyph (HY-ro-glif)—A pictographic symbol used as a form of writing by ancient civilizations.

import (IM-port)—To bring goods in from another country for sale.

indigenous (in-DIJ-uh-nus)—Originally from a particular region.

judicial branch (joo-DISH-ul BRANCH)—The section of government responsible for the administration of justice (upholding laws).

legislative branch (leh-jis-LAY-tiv BRANCH)—The section of government responsible for developing laws.

matador (MAT-uh-dor)—The chief bullfighter who kills the bull at the end of a bullfight.

peninsula (puh-NIN-suh-luh)—A portion of land almost entirely surrounded by water.

siesta (see-ES-tuh)—A midday period of rest, common in Latin America.

INDEX

Tammy Gagne is the author of numerous books for both adults and children, including *What It's Like To Be Sonia Sotomayor* for Mitchell Lane Publishers. Mexico's Yucatán Peninsula is among Tammy's favorite travel destinations. When she isn't traveling, Tammy resides in northern New England with her husband, son, dogs, and parrots.